HOW IT WAS

BRITAIN AT WAR 1939-45

Michael Rawcliffe

B T Batsford Ltd, London

CONTENTS

© Michael Rawcliffe 1992

First published 1992

Photoset by Deltatype Ltd, Ellesmere Port, Cheshire
and printed in Hong Kong
for the publishers
B. T. Batsford Ltd
4 Fitzhardinge Street
London W1H 0AH

A CIP catalogue record for this book is available from the British Library

ISBN 0 7134 6354 6

Cover illustration:
The evacuation of British troops from Dunkirk in 1940. 338,228 men were rescued from the German bombardment in a period of ten days.

In 1989 both the daily and local papers, radio and television contained many items to commemorate the fiftieth anniversary of the start of the Second World War. During the next six years many other anniversaries will take place, such as 1990 the Battle of Britain, 1995 the Allied Victory. Many people will be looking back and recounting what it was like, or what they were doing at a particular point in time. Oral history is a very important source and you should be able to talk to people who still have vivid memories of such events as Evacuation or the Blitz. Some will have been your age during the war.

There are also many museums and sites to visit. In London the National Army Museum and the Imperial War Museum are essential starting points and the latter is particularly good on the Domestic Front. These museums not only contain photographs and artefacts but also sell postcards, posters and documentary packs.

Learn to treat all evidence with caution. Britain was seeking to win a war, and it was essential that the government should keep up the people's morale. In addition a lot was left unsaid in the newspapers, or left deliberately vague so that the enemy would not gain vital information.

Your aim should be twofold. Firstly, to find out what actually happened, and where appropriate, how and why. Secondly, to come to an understanding of the feel of the time. Only then will history come alive.

Introductory Quiz

Do you know?
what the following abbreviations stand for?

ARP	HG
CD	AFS
WVS	NFS

what a utility mark and points rationing were?

who would have said 'Put that light out'?

who said 'This is our finest hour'?

why UXB, V1's and V2's were so feared?

what the Phoney War was?

how the Battle of Britain was won?

As you proceed through the book you should be able to find the solutions to these questions.

On 3 September 1939 Britain and France declared war on Germany, after the Germans had invaded Poland.

But in the summer of 1939, the British Government had moved some 3·5 million people to safer areas. Extensive preparations were made and the country was divided into three areas. London and the cities – the places at greatest risk from bombing – were the evacuation areas. A second category was called neutral areas, which people were not allowed to move into, or depart from. Thirdly, there were the reception areas, where evacuees would be located (see page 20).

Britain was preparing for heavy bombing, which many thought would come as soon as the war commenced. No longer were planes used mainly for reconnaissance or for dropping bombs by hand. By the late 1930s the leading nations had developed heavily armed air forces – the German airforce or *Luftwaffe* was large and equipped with some of the most up-to-date aircraft in the world.

Thus Britain prepared – trenches were dug in major cities, gas masks distributed, Anderson shelters erected, plans made for rationing and voluntary services organized. Both the AFS and ARP were formed prior to the war, which the Government rightly believed would involve not only the Armed Forces, but also the civilian population.

With the declaration of war, Britain prepared for the inevitable bombing of the cities. The Government estimated that some 600,000 civilians would be killed and a quarter of a million would be wounded in the first two months. Thus the WVS was formed to provide support in the event of war. They were to make and distribute clothes and blankets to refugees and provide linen and bandages for hospitals. It was expected that the war would last about three years.

In early September these plans were put into action and within three days of the declaration of war 1·5 million people had left the big cities. Whole schools were despatched with their teachers, and a new word came into common use – evacuee.

Gas masks were issued to everybody and ARP wardens were made responsible for ensuring that people used them properly and carried them at all times. Strangely enough the wearing of them was not compulsory.

In spite of all the preparations very little happened. People began to drift back to their homes, and there was a public reaction against the defence forces, who appeared to be imposing unnecessary regulations when there was no danger. Britain at this time lacked real leadership

SERVE TO SAVE

Air Raid Precautions (ARP) such as the carrying of gas masks and the blackout were enforced by voluntary wardens.

Women played an important role in all the 'auxiliary services'.

and this plus lack of military action led to this early period of the war being given nicknames such as the Phoney War or Bore War.

However, it was not only on the Home Front that little seemed to be happening. In September 1939 the BEF had been despatched across the Channel to help defend France against the expected German attack. This did not happen and troops spent most of their time on sentry duty.

1940 saw the coldest January and February for 45 years, and the Thames froze over a distance of eight miles. This only added to the misery of people now subject to regulations and restrictions.

Only at sea was there a real war. The German battleship *Graf Spee* was sunk and in April 1940 the Allies mined Norwegian waters. This led Hitler to invade Denmark. The Phoney War was over.

A false alarm

Sir Edward Colville wrote in his diary on 3 September 1939:

It was widely believed that London would be reduced to rubble within minutes of war being declared, as recently depicted to an alarmed populace in the film of H. G. Wells' book called *Things to Come*; and it seemed that this was indeed about to happen. So we scuttled to the air-raid shelter. There I played bridge [until] the all-clear sounded, for the sirens had been set off on account of a single unidentified aircraft spotted miles to the east of the Thames estuary.

(E. Colville, *The Fringes of Power*, Vol. I, Hodder and Stoughton, 1985)

Is there anything in this extract and on the previous two pages to suggest why Colville feared the worst when he heard the siren?

Many other authors wrote about the raid on the first day of the war. Do you think that this would be useful to the historian or is it merely giving us information that we already have?

Protection against blast – a suggestion from the Ministry of Home Security.

CHECK YOUR UNDERSTANDING

AFS   Auxiliary Fire Service (the volunteers)

ARP   Air Raid Precautions

BEF   British Expeditionary Force (the regular soldiers sent to France)

WAF   Women's Air Force

WVS   Women's Volunteer Service

Anderson shelter   Shelters provided by the Government to each householder

Armed Forces   The Army, Navy and Air Force

Populace   People

Nurses – and babies – in gas masks.

THINGS TO DO

1 Write a letter to a friend in Canada on the day war broke out, giving your feelings about both the present and the future.

2 The date is 3 September 1939 and you are with a group of friends. Discuss your feelings about the news that Britain is now at war.

3 Which do you think is the best description of this period – Phoney War or Bore War? Explain your choice and say why neither was entirely accurate.

4 In your local library you will find examples of both local and national newspapers from September 1939 and January 1940. Make a note of useful headings and detail.

Why do you think these women entered into this work with such enthusiasm?

A WVS centre

Mrs N. Last describes her work in a WVS centre:

Tuesday, 5 September, 1939

I went to the W.V.S. centre today and was amazed at the huge crowd. We have moved into a big room in the middle of town now, but big as it is, every table was crowded uncomfortably with eager workers. Afterwards, huge stacks of wool to be knitted into bedcovers, and dozens of books of tailors' patterns to be machined together, were taken. They average about 77 yards of machining to join each piece with a double row of stitching and a double-stitched hem. I'm on my third big one and have made about a dozen cot quilts. As my husband says, it would have been quicker to walk the distance than machine it. I'm lucky, for my machine is electric and so does not tire me. Everyone seemed to be so kind.

(N. Last, *Nelly's Last War, A Mother's Diary 1939–45*, Sphere, 1983)

DUNKIRK

With the invasion of Denmark and Norway in April 1940 and France in May 1940, the Phoney War came to an end. The German army swept across Northern France and on 20 May plans were drawn up by Britain for 'an emergency evacuation across the Channel of our troops'. The codename given to the operation was Dynamo. Evacuations were to take place from Calais, Boulogne and Dunkirk at the rate of 10,000 every 24 hours. However, by 26 May both Calais and Boulogne had fallen to the Germans. Soon Dunkirk was full of weary and wounded troops battered constantly by the German artillery as it tightened the noose. The German High Command felt so confident that they announced 'The ring around the British, French and Belgian forces is closed for ever'. Winston Churchill, who had only become Prime Minister on 10 May, told the House of Commons 'to prepare itself for hard and heavy tidings'.

It was now that Operation Dynamo was put into effect. Orders went out for ships and men to supplement the Royal Navy. The response was tremendous and during the period from 26 May to 4 June, 338,226 men were evacuated, far more than the 45,000 it had been thought would be saved.

The Dunkirk coastline is a dangerous one for inexperienced seamen. It is riddled with shoals, sandbanks and narrow passages. This meant that the survivors had to wade or be ferried out to the larger ships from the shallow water.

Fortunately the seas were calm. The people of Kent listened to the German bombardment and watched the flashes on the horizon some 20 miles across the Channel.

The churches, the Salvation Army, the WVS and many other voluntary organizations and individuals responded magnificently. Clothing, especially blankets, was needed and so was food. Each train leaving Dover stopped for eight minutes at the village of Headcorn where local volunteers working from a large barn provided the passengers with food and hot drinks. To save time, litter was thrown out of the train windows to be collected by volunteers before the next train arrived.

The Germans kept up a constant bombardment of Dunkirk. Many British troops wondered why the RAF was not more evident, but their limited resources were used in seeking to prevent more German planes getting to Dunkirk.

The weary returning troops were given a tremendous welcome. Union Jacks were waved and there were many home-made banners bearing the words 'Bravo BEF' and 'Welcome Home'. The

evacuation was welcomed as a victory for freedom. The New York Times in June 1940 wrote:

So long as the English tongue survives, the word Dunkirk will be spoken with reverence. For in that harbour, in such a hell as never blazed on earth before, at the end of a lost battle, the rags and blemishes that have hidden the soul of democracy fell away. There, beaten but unconquered, in shining splendour, she faced the enemy.

The beaches of Dunkirk. In spite of the German onslaught more than 330,000 men were evacuated.

BLACK-OUT 9.34 p.m. to 4.20 a.m.
Sun rises 4.51 a.m.
sets 9.4 p.m.
Moon rises 2.44 a.m. turn
sets 4.12 p.m.

KING LEOPOLD DETHRONED: Page Three

Have a **CAPSTAN** – they're blended better 1/4¹ for 20 8¹ for 10

Daily Sketch

DAILY SKETCH, FRIDAY, MAY 31, 1940

MILITARY PICKLE THREE SIZES 7d.1'·&18 *The Great Digestive*

No. 9,693 (E**) FRIDAY, MAY 31, 1940 ONE PENNY

MANY B.E.F. TROOPS BROUGHT OUT

In Scores of Ships—Paddle Boats, Cargo Boats, 'Tramps,' Barges

Here are some of the men of the B.E.F., whose perilous journey home from Flanders is told to-day. British, French and Belgian soldiers have come across in scores of ships—paddle-boats, cargo-boats, tramp steamers and even barges. Almost every ship was bombed by German dive bombers.

Coast Battle Raging: Dunkirk Held: Nazis Claim French General Captured

Full Story, Page Three : See Also Sir Philip Gibbs's Dispatch, Page Two

Boats used in the evacuation from Dunkirk

5031 in 203 private motor boats
4895 in 27 yachts (some of them manned by the Royal Navy)
28,709 in 230 trawlers and drifters
48,472 in 38 minesweepers
87,910 in 45 assorted vessels manned by the Royal Navy and Merchant Navy
102,843 in 56 destroyers and torpedo boats.

NB. These are only the larger categories of boats and exclude some of those mentioned on the previous page.

(Source: P. Fleming, *Invasion 1940*, Hamish Hamilton, 1958)

Why do you think the destroyers and torpedo boats managed to bring over so many survivors?

The Dunkirk retreat was treated almost as a victory.

CHECK YOUR UNDERSTANDING

Artillery Heavy guns used in the assault on Dunkirk

Cockle A small fishing boat

Coxswain The man who steers a boat

DSM Distinguished Service Medal

Naval rating A sailor in the Royal Navy

Salvation Army A Christian group founded by William Booth in the 19th century

Southern Railway One of the railway companies before the railways were taken over by the State

Wherry [ies] A shallow light boat, rather like a barge

Bravery

Coxswain Knight and his crew took the Ramsgate lifeboat across to Dunkirk on the afternoon of Thursday 30 May 1940 towing eight wherries manned by naval ratings and loaded with cans of fresh water for the troops. They were at work all the Thursday night, the Friday and Friday night and continued until all the wherries were destroyed. They helped to bring off 2800 men in forty hours. Coxswain Parker and the Margate crew also set out on the Thursday afternoon and arrived at the beaches at midnight. They rescued first a party of French soldiers, who waded out to the lifeboat in the darkness, and by 8.30 next morning had brought off five to six hundred men.

(Source: A. Roots, *Front Line County: Kent at War 1939–45*, Hale, 1980)

THINGS TO DO

1 You are living in a Kentish village. Discuss with your neighbour what you can organize to help the incoming soldiers.

2 You have experienced the evacuation from Dunkirk. Describe how you were rescued.

3 Today people still talk of the 'Dunkirk Spirit'. From what you have read, explain why this is so.

4 In many ways Dunkirk was a defeat. Why then do we regard it as a victory?

The Coxswain was awarded the DSM. What particular bravery did he and his crew show?

CAN YOU REMEMBER ?

when the Phoney War was said to have ended?

why Dunkirk was chosen rather than Boulogne or Calais?

Dunkirk evacuees being fed at Headcorn Station, Kent.

THE BATTLE OF BRITAIN

After the defeat of the Allied forces in Europe and the evacuation from Dunkirk, Britain stood alone. It was widely believed that Hitler would now seek to invade and thus complete his conquest of Western Europe.

On 2 August 1940 Goering called for the destruction of the RAF and the emphasis of the attack was now changed from attacks on coastal shipping to bombing the ports of Southern England. Massed formations of bombers (mainly Junker dive bombers) were escorted by large fighter formations flying above them. The RAF responded with Spitfires and Hurricanes, which were heavily outnumbered by the Luftwaffe. Many people watched as battles were fought out daily in the skies above them. The Luftwaffe outnumbered the RAF by 3:1, but the RAF were fighting 'at home' and the Luftwaffe BF 109s had only 30 minutes over land before their fuel was exhausted.

At first Goering hoped that the RAF would be drawn into attacking the fighters guarding the bombers. In this way he hoped that Britain's fighter strength would be so weakened that victory would be assured. However, the British Commanders Dowding and Park held off and concentrated on attacking the bombers. Thus the myth of the Battle of Britain mainly consisting of heroic dogfights is not the case. In fact Britain's problems were less the loss of aircraft than the loss of pilots, and many raw recruits were pitted against the more experienced German pilots, many of whom had gained their battle experience in the Spanish Civil War.

By mid August Goering realized that his tactics must be changed. More fighter cover was provided for the heavy bombers, and later faster bombers were substituted.

Radar played a decisive part in Britain's defences, and when they were breached the Royal Army Ordnance Corps (RAOC) tracked the planes with binoculars from various lookouts. On the ground the army, the anti-aircraft guns, the barrage balloons and the large number of volunteers all played their part.

A flight of Spitfires.

Battle of Britain pilots.

On the night of 24 August several German pilots lost their way and, unable to find the aircraft factories and oil refineries, bombed Central London by mistake. Churchill ordered a reprisal raid, and Berlin was bombed four days later. Again there was an error and civilian areas were bombed as well as military ones. The German public was shocked, as Hitler had promised that this would never happen. The German retaliation was sharp – at the end of August Liverpool was bombed and some 160 fires lit the skyline. Hitler was still not satisfied and on Saturday, 7 September one hundred bombers broke through British defences, reaching the London Docks at 5 p.m. Incendiaries were dropped, which guided in the bombers. The raid continued until 4.30 a.m. the next morning. In spite of the loss of life and casualties, Britain held firm. Operation Sea Lion could not be put into effect as the Luftwaffe had not gained control of the skies. In this sense Britain had won the Battle of Britain.

On 17 September the German invasion plan was postponed indefinitely and Hitler began his preparations for the invasion of Russia. Meanwhile the British public became more united against Germany. Britain had entered the next phase of the war – the Blitz – which was to last until May 1941.

BATTLE OF BRITAIN

Battle losses 1 July – 31 October, 1940

	RAF	Luftwaffe
Lost, missing or destroyed	892	1492
Lost in accidents	221	184

How to recognize the enemy – silhouettes of German bombers.

Q

What comments would you make about these figures? Why did the Luftwaffe lose more planes in action and the RAF more in accidents?

Junkers 88

This is a comparatively small fast bomber and reconnaissance machine (similar to our "Blenheim"). It is powered with two 1,100 h.p. Jumo motors and carries a crew of three, and three machine guns. A more recent model, the Ju. 88K, is supposed to have a top speed of about 300 m.p.h. and a range of 1,300 miles; so the performance of the Ju. 88 is almost certainly quite a bit lower. Distinctive features are the short nose—shorter than is usual on German aircraft of this type, the way the engine nacelles hang below the wing, and the straight lines of the fuselage when seen from the side. The break in the trailing edge towards the wing tips is also distinctive, and the fuselage projects slightly beyond the rudder.

Dornier 215

This is one of the latest Nazi bombers, known as the "Flying Pencil," from its slim profile. It has a top speed of 292 m.p.h. and a range of 1,490 miles. Latest models have 1,100 h.p. inverted vee twelve-cylinder Daimler-Benz engines. Span is 59ft. 3in. and length 55ft. 5in. A bomb load of 1,500lb. is carried inside the fuselage. The machine carries three guns, one in a turret underneath, and is operated by a crew of three. An earlier version, the Do. 17, has a speed of 260 m.p.h. and a prominent top turret, but is "blind" underneath, as some of our fighter pilots have discovered. Chief features are the twin rudders, semi-circular wing tips, slender rear fuselage, and a comparatively bulky nose. It is about the same length as our "Hampden," but the span is nearer that of the "Blenheim."

CHECK YOUR UNDERSTANDING

Herman Goering Head of the Luftwaffe

Hurricane A British fighter plane. Maximum speed 328 MPH; max. range 505 miles, 8 machine guns mounted in the wings

Junker A German bomber. 3 guns front and rear. Bomb-load 3968 lbs. Max. speed 286 MPH; max. range 1553 miles

Luftwaffe the German Air Force

Messersmitt German fighter plane. Max. speed 357 MPH. Max. range 412 miles. 4 machine guns

Operation Sea Lion The German plan for the invasion of Britain

Radar The use of high-powered radio pulses for locating planes, or determining one's own position. Name derived from R(adio) D(etection) R(anging)

RAOC The Royal Army Ordnance Corps

Reprisal To retaliate, or get one's own back

Spitfire British fighter plane. Max. speed 362 MPH. Range 395 miles. 8 machine guns

THINGS TO DO

1 The leading planes used in the Battle of Britain were Messersmitts, Spitfires, Hurricanes, Dorniers, Junkers and Heinkels. Using other reference books divide them into British and German, fighter and bomber, and try to find out about the strengths and limitations of each.

2 In pairs imagine that you are on the ground watching a dogfight taking place above you. Describe what you see.

3 You are stationed at a major aerodrome and are awaiting your first mission. The alarm goes and the enemy has been picked up by radar heading northwards towards London. Continue the story through to your safe return.

4 Look at the evidence on these pages. Why is the Battle of Britain seen as a victory?

A Heinkel over London.

THE BLITZ

September 1940 saw the beginning of one of the worst periods of the war for the civilian population – the Blitz. It is interesting that the British public adopted this German word for the night raids which were launched on London and all the major cities, from September 1940 to the end of May 1941.

Goering's change of tactics from mainly daytime air raids was in part due to the failure of the Luftwaffe to win the Battle of Britain. Now the civilian population, as well as strategic sites (such as factories and barracks), were to be attacked without mercy.

The first severe raid began on 7 September 1940 on the East End of London. Considerable damage was done not only to the Docks, but also to the many terraced houses. There followed two months of almost continuous bombing, with approximately 160 German bombers shedding their load each night.

Against all expectations morale did not collapse. In fact, once over the initial shock, people returned to work, and production in the factories was not reduced. People came to take pride in making do and carrying on as normal, in far from normal circumstances. Rather than morale falling, the spirit of camaraderie resulting from the bombing brought people of all classes together as never before.

Of course there are many myths about the Blitz. Not everyone was able to cope and adapt to a destroyed house or lost loved one, and the incessant bombing night after night. But sufficient people did. At first people did not go out, but in time they returned to their 'normal' lives in spite of the Blackout, disrupted transport, broken gas and water mains, or no electricity. For many shops 'Business as Usual' was their brave notice displayed in a window often without its glass.

Warning of an air raid was by the Alert – the wail of a siren rising and falling for two minutes. This was a sound which once heard one would never forget. In these two minutes people would seek safety in a cellar, under the stairs, under the kitchen table, or in their own Anderson Shelter in the garden. If they were outside they would go to a public shelter. In Chislehurst in Kent thousands were admitted nightly to the famous caves, whilst in London many slept on the platforms of the London Underground (the Tube). Wherever you were you would hear the throb of the approaching bombers, then would come the parachute flares, amber or green, to make the bombing easier. Finally would come the bombs, when everything would shake and rattle and you would listen to the bombs raining down hoping that 'your number

was not on it' as the soldiers at the front used to say. Finally would come the All Clear – a two minute blast on the siren. People emerged to carry on living their lives as best they could. This was repeated night after night. People would go about their work during the day and then many would help in the various voluntary services at night – in the AFS, the Home Guard, as air raid wardens, or as street wardens.

St Paul's Cathedral rises above blitzed London.

On duty in North London

An ARP Warden in North London reported on 17 September 1940:

I was on duty at the post with Mr K (age 35) when the explosions occurred.

There was a sudden rushing sound – not a whistle – and Mr K just had time to exclaim 'That's close!' – when three loud explosions shook the room, and we heard some screams from a neighbouring house. We rush out into the road, and find ourselves on the edge of a dense cloud of dust. One could feel the separate particles tingling against one's face, and it was difficult to breathe or see anything. A man (about 30) rushes from the other side of the road yelling to us:

'You can't go down there, there's a bomb. You can't go down there. There are bombs. You can't go down there!'

We push past him and plunge into the cloud of dust. It is a lovely moonlit night, but here it is impossible to see. A strong smell of coal-gas directs us across Abbey Road to the lower half of Boundary Road; and after about 40 yards we find ourselves on the edge of a crater about 15 feet across, exactly in the middle of the road. Boulders of clay have been thrown up all round, and there is a rushing sound of water and a greatly intensified smell of coal-gas. Mr K has the report forms, and begins filling one up *in the dark*, while I stumble about trying to find out if there are casualties.

(Source: T. Harrison, *Living through the Blitz*, Penguin, 1978)

Q

What are the dangers of damage to gas and water supplies?
Why did Mr K start filling in the report forms so quickly?

A London bus almost submerged in a bomb crater.

Bomb damage to houses in Poplar, east London.

THINGS TO DO

1 There is still plenty of visual evidence of the Blitz. If you live in London or its suburbs, or in a town, it is likely that you will find signs of roof damage, or gaps in older terraced roads where now houses have been built.

2 Talk to older people about their war experiences. Record what they say and see whether it compares with diaries which were kept at the time.

3 How would your morale have stood up to nightly bombing? Write an imaginary diary in which your house was bombed or suffered blast damage.

Your local library will be able to give you information about which areas suffered during the Blitz.

Damage to a house in Barrow

Sunday, 4 May 1941

A night of terror, and there are few windows left in the district – or roof tiles! Land mines, incendiaries and explosives were dropped, and we cowered thankfully under our indoor shelter. I've been so dreadfully sick all day, and I'm sure it's sheer fright, for last night I really thought our end had come. By the time the boys come, I'll be able to laugh about it. Now I've a sick shadow over me as I look at my loved little house that will never be the same again. The windows are nearly all out, the metal frames strained, the ceilings down, the walls cracked and the garage roof showing four inches of daylight where it joins the wall. Doors are splintered and off – and there is the *dirt* from the blast that swept down the chimney. The house rocked, and then the kitchenette door careered down the hall and plaster showered on to the shelter. I'll never forget my odd sensations, one a calm acceptance of 'the end', the other a feeling of regret that I'd not opened a tin of fruit salad for tea – and now it was too late!

(N. Last, *Nelly Last's War: A Mother's Diary 1939–45*, Sphere, 1983)

Q

The diary was written at the time. What are the feelings of the lady after the damage to her house?

EVACUATION

As war drew near in August 1939 the Government began to put into operation its defence measures. On the last day of August the voluntary evacuation of children of school age from danger areas took place (see *Phoney War*, page 4).

In the first phase roughly half of London's schoolchildren were evacuated. The day of departure must have been very painful for both parents and children. In the early morning the children were lined up in the playground by their teachers. Each child carried a gas mask and a bag containing essential items. Some children were said to have departed with buckets and spades because their parents had not the heart to tell them what was really happening. Another story was that a child asked why the mothers at the school gate were crying, to which a quick-witted teacher replied, 'Because they cannot go on their holidays, too'.

The children, walking in pairs, were led to the station by a person – usually the school caretaker – carrying a placard giving the reference number of the group. The majority of children departed by train and in four days 72 London Transport Stations despatched some 1.3 million children in 4000 special trains.

Often the trains were diverted along branch lines. Many only had single compartments and no corridors. The only food was that which was taken and toilet facilities were few. The journey was often long, and no one on board, not even the teachers, knew where they were going. On arrival, the children were marched to the reception centre, which was often a school or a church hall. Then began the long process of distributing children among the local people. Once settled, parents would visit their children at the weekend, but by the end of the year, with the expected bombing not having taken place, many parents took their children home.

When the Blitz began the process began again, and this time the Government began to clear all children from a belt ten miles inland from the coasts of Norfolk and Suffolk and later from towns such as Chatham, Rochester, Hull and Portsmouth.

The other form of evacuation consisted of institutions such as schools, hospitals and government departments being relocated in safer areas. Hospitals in the towns and cities were cleared of patients so that they could accommodate war casualties. Many large country houses and mental hospitals were requisitioned and doctors and nurses despatched to them to await the injured.

The BBC moved to Bristol, and then, when Bristol was bombed, to Evesham in Worcestershire. Billingsgate Fish Market left London for Maidstone, while part of the War Office went to Evesham, and part of the Ministry of Information to Malvern. Civil servants from London were dispersed as far away as Blackpool in Lancashire and many remained in their new homes after the war ended.

Many who could afford to left the danger areas voluntarily. Several of the coastal towns of the South East and their populations fell dramatically. Folkestone in Kent saw its population of 46,000 drop to 6000.

Fear of the bombing of civilian targets by the Germans led the authorities to evacuate children from cities to the country.

Looking for a house

George Beardsmore had moved to Droitwich with the BBC, leaving a wife and child in a London suburb. He kept a record of events between 1938 and 1946.

14 October 1940

My chief concern, now that the office is in full swing again and likely to stay here, is to find a home for Jean and the infant. But because the engineers have been here before me, homes are as easy to find as jobs pre-war. But I must get those two out of Harrow. We learn that St Mary's spire has been toppled, that Colindale Under-ground station has been put out of action, and that a bomb has contrived to land on a Piccadilly escalator. One begins to see why in these parts the war is treated as a rather unpleasant newspaper serial. Have answered advertisements and toured the countryside on the bike, as also my residential quarter of Droitwich. Five of the engineers, and my immediate boss Fletcher, are like-wise on the prowl.

(G. Beardsmore, *Civilians at War: Journal 1938–44*, OUP 1984)

Q

Why would being in Droitwitch make things even worse for George Beardsmore?

Evacuees from Bristol on their way to Devon.

THINGS TO DO

1   Find out whether your school was evacuated *or* if your school was in a reception area and whether it had to share with another school from an evacuation area. The school may have a Log Book (an official diary kept by the Head) from the time which gives details. If material is available, try to work out a story or a play in which you were either evacuated with your school, or had evacuees coming to your school.

2   Your grandparents may have memories of evacuation. Ask them to describe their experiences and what it felt like. Draw up headings for the interview such as the day we left home, the journey, arrival, my new school, life in the area, and my new home.

3   How do you think you would have coped in a new school, in a different area? Many things, such as local accents, would have been quite different. Try to record your thoughts in diary form and compare them with what people can tell you about how they actually felt.

Evacuation from a child's point of view

I was a child of six in Portsmouth when heavy bombing took place on the dockyard, and I was evacuated with my brother and sister to the country in Surrey. We were split up and sent to different billets. I was put into a large home for evacuees, where I stayed for eight months over the winter. Every day we had three pieces of bread and margarine for breakfast and supper, and a boiled potato with thin gravy for lunch. There was no heating and when the pipes froze we did not wash. I wanted to get back home so I ran away with two small friends. After walking two miles we were discovered and taken back. I was caned several times in front of the whole school for being a naughty girl.

Not all memories were bad. The same lady's husband was sent from Portsmouth to an aunt in the north of Scotland.

I enjoyed the war despite the abrupt change imposed. I spent my school holidays in the hills and woods playing. I have never lost my love for Scotland and the countryside.

London evacuees digging a vegetable patch.

The threat of invasion and the bombing gave virtually everyone the opportunity to help in the war effort and feel that they were being useful.

The Government's preparations against possible air attack had begun long before the war actually started, and continued steadily as the European crisis developed. In 1938 some 38 million gas masks were distributed by volunteers mainly drawn from the WVS, the Red Cross and the Boy Scouts. Thus when war broke out in September 1939 local authorities had already drawn up their plans for Civil Defence (as required by the Air Raid Precautions Act of 1937).

The main person associated with ARP was the warden. In spite of the fact that he was often the butt of humour, he played an essential role. In each local area there was a chief warden, with responsibility for the wardens under him. Some were full-time and paid, and both men and women could apply. The familiar blue serge suit, overcoat, beret or tin helmet and boots were not officially distributed until 1941. Others were part-timers who did their duties after work.

The wardens were the eyes and ears of the whole Civil Defence mechanism. Their duties included going to an incident and reporting to the Control Post, putting out minor fires, giving first aid, directing people to shelters at the start of an air raid, investigating UXBs and generally enforcing regulations. The latter essential duty often earned the warden the nickname of 'Little Hitler', as he could report people for inadequate blackout or leaving lights exposed which could be seen from the sky. ('Put that light out!') The good warden knew everyone within his area. It was essential that he knew whether they were day or night workers, and which bedroom each person slept in, in order to make rescue easier and to avoid wasteful searches of the debris of a house looking for survivors who might not be there.

Other essential workers were the AFS who gave part-time assistance to the full-time professional firemen. Before the war there was often friction between these two groups, as the full-time workers were poorly paid, but during the Battle of Britain the AFS proved their worth and gave invaluable service. Many lost their lives dealing with the multitudes of fires and collapsed

Incendiary bombs were a particular hazard.

buildings, and all firemen earned the respect of everyone.

The Blitz stretched the Civil Defence forces to the limit and in 1940 Fire Watchers were formed. At first every business and factory had to choose workers to watch the buildings at weekends and at night. Their only equipment was a bucket and a stirrup pump. In December 1940 every man working less than 60 hours a week and every woman doing less than 45 had to do 48 hours firewatching a month. By 1943 there were six milion firewatchers, all of whom were unpaid.

The list of essential volunteers is endless. For example, office workers manned the Civil Defence Headquarters which controlled the various services once an attack took place. They would determine the severity of an incident and which services should be sent – fire, ambulance, and so on.

Groups of gas, water, electrical and post office engineers were kept on permanent alert so that they could repair essential services. The Auxiliary Police Corps (APC) were the volunteers who assisted the overstretched Police Force. Many women acted as drivers, telephonists, nurses and in other important areas.

The Red Cross and the St John's Ambulance Brigade gave valuable medical and nursing assistance at the local level, while the WVS helped administer evacuation, provided tea and refreshments for the homeless, organized clothes collection and ran charities.

In fact, everyone had a vital part to play.

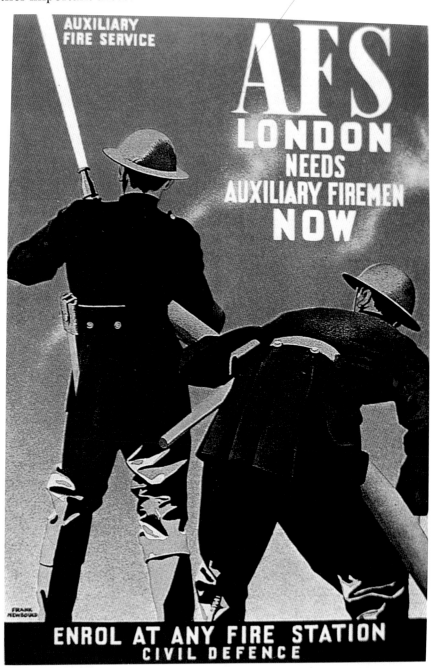

Recruitment poster for the Auxiliary Fire Service.

An ARP Warden with a stirrup pump.

Don't lose your sense of proportion

Keep cheerful yourself, and keep others cheerful too.

A long face does not help anyone, but a cheerful face always makes the day seem brighter.

Do you go 'sightseeing' after an air raid?

Don't do this. You don't mean to be thoughtless, but an influx of people in a bombed area hinders the work of the Services and makes things more difficult for the workers who have to get to and from their jobs.

A sudden increase in numbers in an area, all wanting something to eat, and drink, may mean that when tired A.R.P. workers come off duty there is nothing left for them.

Do you rush out to see what has happened if a bomb falls in your neighbourhood?

Do not do this. Although people are always eager to help when such things happen, crowds only hinder the work of the Civil Defence forces.

(C. Atkinson, *ARP at Home: Hints for Housewives*, HMSO, 1941)

Which of the pieces of advice would you have found most difficult to put into practice?

THINGS TO DO

1 The alert has sounded. Look at the various Civil Defence groups mentioned in this section. What would each have had to do?

2 Check copies of your local newspaper published during the war for references to the various Civil Defence groups and note down any reports that you find.

3 Do you know anyone who served in Civil Defence during the war? If so, talk to them about their experiences. Try and find out how your street or area was organized against attack.

CHECK YOUR UNDERSTANDING

What do the following abbreviations mean?

ARP, WVS, AFS.

Can you guess what UXB was?

A Look at a Control Room

Blackpool in Lancashire saw very little bombing, but every town had to be prepared. A reporter observed an exercise at the Civil Defence No. 1 Control Room in 1943:

> When one analyses the staff, it is revealed that every branch of Civil Defence is represented in the room — police, fire service, rescue and demolition, first aid, messengers, gas, wardens, ambulance.

Men, women and girls were in the midst of a battery of telephones, pencils, sheets of paper, maps and lettered and numbered discs.

Telephones rang almost incessantly. Messages were received and despatched. It was a hive of activity. Each had a job to do, and did it in a calm, confident, and orderly manner.

(*The Gazette and Herald*, 13 February 1943)

Nowhere in the article is the location of the Control Room mentioned. Why is this?

Look at the organizations mentioned in the second paragraph. Why would each have been represented?

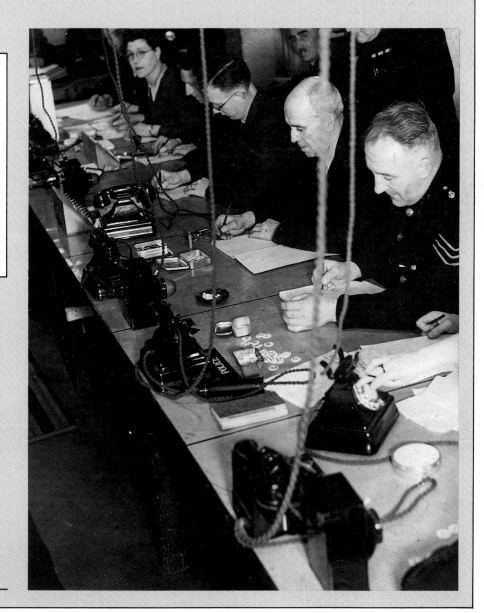

Civil Defence Control Room, Blackpool.

Germany invaded the Low Countries on 10 May 1940 and a few days later in a radio broadcast Anthony Eden, the Secretary of State for War, called for a Local Defence Volunteer Force (LDV). Before the broadcast was over men were volunteering, and within 24 hours a quarter of a million men had come forward. By mid-July the numbers had risen to a million.

In August 1940 Winston Churchill renamed them the Home Guard (HG). Those who have seen excerpts from the old television comedy series 'Dad's Army' will imagine that they were rather a joke. On screen they seem to consist of pleasant – even eccentric – old men, who could have contributed little to the defence of the country.

At first the Home Guard had no uniforms and little equipment; in Kent, at first, they had only one rifle between ten men. They were regarded as inferior to the Civil Defence which was formally organized by the local authorities. At first they wore armbands, but soon they were linked to their county regiments and could wear their colours and cap badges. Equally their makeshift weapons soon became a thing of the past, but the Home Guard always remained very regional. On Lake Windermere they manned motor vessels, while in Devon, Cornwall and Wales many of the Home Guard used horses.

As time passed, the structure became more formal. Men between 17 and 65 were allowed to join, though unofficially the age limits were often breached. From February 1942 every male was obliged to join, if he was not already in the Armed Forces or in Civil Defence. Every recruit was required to do 48 hours unpaid service per month. Training was on military lines and took place after work and at weekends.

How far the Home Guard would have provided a real defence in the event of invasion is doubtful. On the other hand their importance was recognized by the enemy. Hitler dubbed them 'a murder gang', though what probably concerned him was that they went on patrol, kept watch and guard, supporting the Regular Army and the Police. Without the Home Guard the Army would have had to use valuable men to watch over 5000 miles of coastline. One of the Home Guard's

greatest successes was in capturing Hitler's second in command, Rudolf Hess, when he landed in Scotland during the war.

The composition of the Home Guard represented all sections of society. On the one hand there were ex-officers, who continued to wear their ranks from the Armed Forces. On the other were those who were still in their last year of school. As one of the extracts on the next page shows, experience was the key – and frequently the man with war experience would be in command of those without. Thus it was possible on occasions for a worker to be in command of his boss.

Founded in May 1940 the Local Defence Volunteers (later renamed the Home Guard) had 1·5 million recruits within a month.

"Let 'em all come"

MEN 41-55

HOME DEFENCE BATTALIONS

Apply at any Army Recruiting Centre Now

'SPOT AT SIGHT' CHART №· 1
ENEMY UNIFORMS

GERMAN PARACHUTIST

GERMAN SOLDIER

A Home Guard training exercise.

On the Golf Course

Heavier weapons, like the Northover grenade projector were tried out on Sundridge Park Golf Course – where a cry of 'fore' required special heeding. Field exercises were treated very seriously: the 'enemy' not infrequently being highly trained infantry regulars.

(L. Blake, *Bromley in the Front Line*, Private publication, 1980)

Which of these extracts support the statement that the Home Guard should be taken seriously? Can you guess what civvies were and what NCO stands for?

The BBC Home Guard

How odd it seemed to see some of the higher officers of the Corporation being ordered about and instructed in the use of the rifle by the Commissioners [doormen] who had earlier addressed them with 'Good morning, Sir!' when they walked in, umbrellas folded neatly, to start a day's administration.

(W. Pickles, *Between You and Me,* Werner Laurie, 1949)

The Home Guard in West London

In one room a Home Guard armourer was busy overhauling rifles and machine guns. In another an unarmed combat expert was teaching the novices how to make others fall and also how to fall themselves. . . . In the largest classroom (they were on the top floor of a school) fifty or sixty men in uniform were doing drill and doing it with a click, in a small one a machine-gun team were stripping and assembling their weapons, while (in another room) a squad of recruits in civvies were learning their first lessons under a patient but strict NCO.

(A. G. Street, *From Dusk till Dawn,* Blandford, 1947)

THINGS TO DO

1   Your local library should give you details of the Home Guard units which operated in your area. Try and find out which places would have been guarded (e.g. a river-crossing or a railway station) and whether they were involved in any reported incidents.

2   Given the evidence in this section, which nickname is most suited to the Home Guard – People's Army or Dad's Army? Give reasons for your answer.

3   If you had a free choice, which voluntary group would you have chosen to join? Give reasons for your choice.

Members of the Home Guard in Orpington, Kent.

CHILDREN AT WAR

Those who were of school age during the war had very varied experiences of 1939–45. At one level there was a mixture of fear and excitement. Fear in the early days at the height of the bombing, hearing about the near miracle of Dunkirk or admiring the fighter pilots of the Battle of Britain who fought virtually single-handed against the enemy.

Fears were often translated into humour. Hitler and his henchmen became figures of fun and playground rhymes abounded, while at side shows and fairs pictures of the Nazi leaders were painted on boards which had to be kicked down by aspiring footballers.

Of course attitudes towards the war varied from family to family. If a father or uncle was on active service, there was always fear when he was posted abroad. Every parent or wife dreaded the telegram announcing that their son or husband had been killed, or was missing on active service. Families might also suffer deaths or injuries in an air raid.

Those children living in cities and ports knew about the war at home at first hand. Some were evacuated to unfamiliar places where many things, such as the local housing and accents, were very different. Some children from the poorest homes in the slums had rarely had a bath and were wrapped in brown paper to keep warm in winter. They were quite unused to having a bedroom of their own, using toothpaste, or sitting down at the table for a meal. Equally, the children of the home to which they were sent probably had their own worries and feelings about their parents' new lodgers.

Living in areas that were constantly being bombed would have been – at the least – very unsettling. Going into the Anderson Shelter in the

A soldier on leave with his daughter at a London swimming pool.

garden, down into the cellar, or merely under the stairs each night might have had its own excitement – as well as fear. In London, many families went each night into the Underground and slept on the platform. Some children counted the benefits. If a raid continued to a certain time, morning school could be missed. Something really serious might lead to permission not to attend at all.

For Bob Crampsey (see the next page) who lived in Glasgow during the war, the main complaint was that the war disrupted the Scottish Football League. For many other people the war was made more real and frightening by the fact that it could be listened to on the radio and watched on the cinema screen for the first time.

A child's collection of wartime cigarette cards and badges.

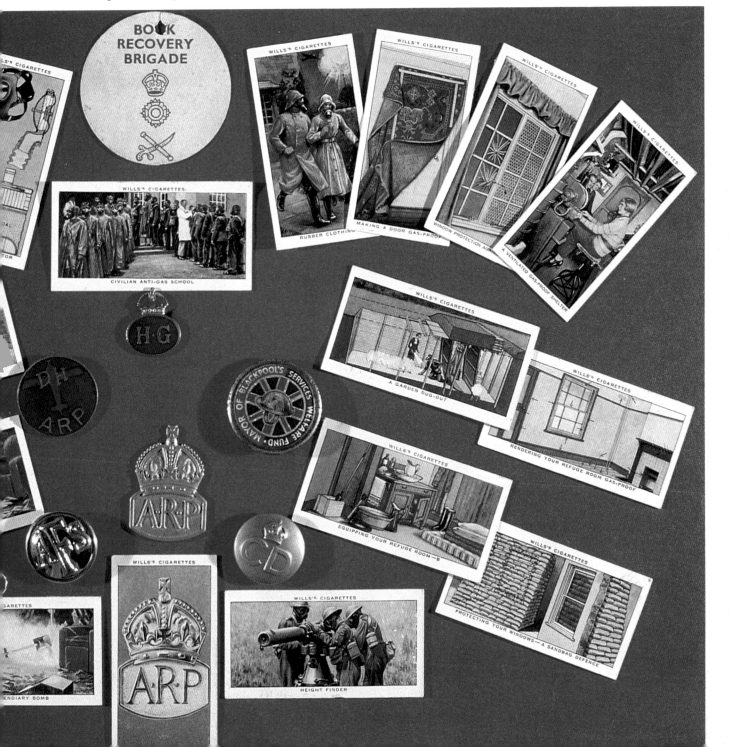

Glasgow in Autumn 1939

Bob Crampsey was nine when the war began.

The uneventful nature of those first few months was something of a real disappointment and we felt vaguely let down by the Germans. What was the point of a war when nothing was happening? There were signs that we were at war, our windows were crisscrossed with paper strips as a protection against blast and black-out material for curtains was bought in hundreds of yards. We carried our gas-masks everywhere and our young sister, Julie, had a Mickey Mouse model which was somehow far more horrific than the orthodox kind, but not much was happening. Cinemas and football grounds were shut and we seemed much more likely to die of boredom rather than at the hands of the enemy.

Look back to the section on the Phoney War. Do you think this extract supports the view that the Bore War was a suitable phrase for this time?

The weather was marvellously warm and we played in the streets, singing the songs of the time, *Run Rabbit Run* and *The Siegfried Line*.

(B. Crampsey, *The Young Civilian: A Glasgow Wartime Childhood*, Headline, 1987)

THINGS TO DO

1 See if you can borrow objects which could be labelled and displayed in an exhibition on 'A Child in the War'. You may be able to borrow badges, books, medals and old newspapers, but make sure that you take good care of them and return them when you have finished.

2 Talking to people who lived through the war can help you to recreate what it was like. In an interview it is a good idea to use photographs which can trigger off memories of the time.

3 Construct either a diary or a log book for your school for a particular time in the war. Your choice will depend on what you have found out about your area. Try and make it as 'real' as possible.

Teacher and pupils wearing gas masks.

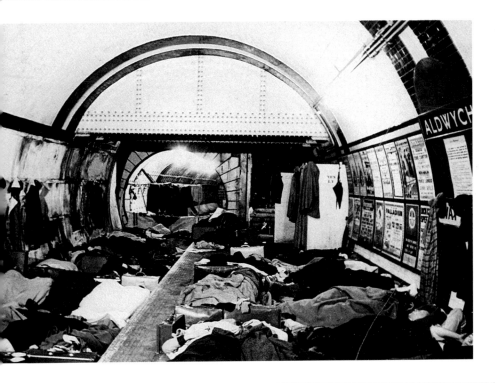

Families slept in London Underground stations to avoid the bombing.

Q

What do you think the knitted comforts (December 23) might have been?
What did the Headteacher mean by native children?

Boughton Monchelsea School during the war

The log book of this Kent Junior school gives a picture of how the war affected the school.

September 19, 1939

During the holidays the Govt. declared war and the main room was commandeered as a First Aid Post and Cleansing Dpt. This necessitated various structural alterations.

The evacuation of Plumstead Timbercraft Junior School also caused re-organization of classes. Three Junior classes of native children under Miss Longman.

October 12, 1939

Air-raid warning in the afternoon. School carried on normally but owing to lost play, dismissed at 3.30 p.m.

December 23, 1939

During the week, a carol party of native children and evacuated children collected £6.11.5. for a wool fund — girls to make knitted comforts for men serving in the forces.

August 16, 1940

In spite of letters from Hd Teacher, Managers and Parents, the K.E.C. have done nothing yet to the School to afford protection against air-raids. During air-raids this week the fall of bombs and the rattle of machine guns could be heard distinctly. Many enemy aircraft have passed over the School.

December 23, 1942

At 11.45 a.m. the School assembled to present Mrs B. B. Jolly (Red Cross) with the money received for the collection of 14 cwt waste paper and fifteen shillings from an afternoon concert. The money she had received she was sending to The Prisoner of War Fund.

DPt	Department
Govt	Government
KEC	Kent Education Committee

RATIONING AND SHORTAGE

During the First World War, food distribution was poor and there were real shortages. At one stage Britain came within six weeks of starvation. In the Second World War rationing was introduced much earlier and the whole operation was regarded as successful.

It was organized by the Ministry of Food, which employed 50,000 civil servants. They were responsible for the buying of all animals, milk and all imported basic foodstuffs. Throughout the country there were over 1000 Food Offices which distributed Ration Books, identity cards, and orange juice and cod liver oil for the young. They were the largest 'shop' in the country and their turnover ran into millions of pounds each year.

The key to the whole operation was the Ration Book. Each Ration Book was a way of measuring out one person's supply of basic foods for a year. Each page was divided into several squared sections. They were of different values (points), and would be initialled with an indelible pen, by the shopkeeper, to show that they had been used.

The items which were first rationed were as follows. Note that, with the exception of meat, they were rationed by weight.

1940 Jan.	Bacon, ham and butter	4oz per week (just over 100 grams)
	Sugar	12oz per week (just over 300 grams)
March	Meat	1/10d (9p) per head for adults
July	Tea, margarine and cooking fats	2oz per week
1941 March	Jam, mince, syrup, marmalade and honey	4oz per week
	Cheese	1oz per week

On 1 December 1941, Points Rationing was introduced. Each adult was allocated 16 points a month (later 20) to spend on the foods of their choice.

Some items were never rationed. Fish, vegetables and sausages were exempted and huge queues developed whenever it was rumoured that a fresh supply had come in. The Ministry of Food sought to encourage people to experiment and several different types of fish went on sale.

Eggs were scarce because there were fewer hens. From 1942 dried egg powder was introduced, as was dried milk. In many ways these were bargains, for mixed with water they provided substantial quantities, at a time when milk was rationed to 2½ pints each week and each person was on average eating only one egg every fortnight.

A National Loaf was introduced, and people had to adjust to a grey loaf made from less-refined flour. Lord Woolton, the Minister for Food, did a magnificent job publicizing the changes, and the need for them. Potato Pete became a popular cartoon character, and carrots were suggested to have qualities which enabled you to see better in the dark.

Newsreels at the cinema had Food Flashes while the Kitchen Front provided housewives with ideas for making the best use of the rations.

Perhaps the best evidence of the success of the food policy was that no one starved. In fact, on average people ate better than before the war and nutritionally the wartime diet was a great improvement, as people found themselves eating more vegetables and less sugar, chocolate and cakes.

Clothes were also rationed and each adult received 66 coupons for 15 months. A woollen dress needed 11 points, and a lined woollen overcoat 18.

Of course there was a black market and 'spivs' made a lot of money illegally. Some scarce items were available 'under the counter' for friends, or for a higher price, but these were the exceptions in a highly successful scheme.

Resources were limited so people were encouraged to 'make-do and mend'.

Go through your wardrobe

Make-do and Mend

DONIA NACHSHEN

BOARD OF TRADE

PRINTED FOR H.M. STATIONERY OFFICE BY W. R. ROYLE & SON LTD., LONDON, E.C.4 51-5556.

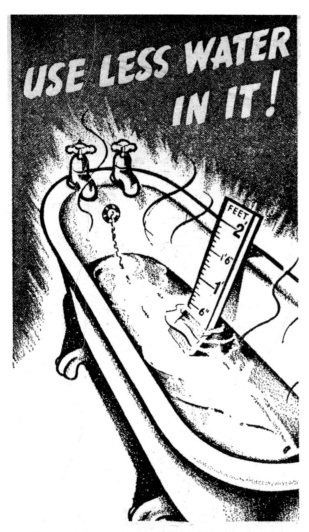

USE LESS WATER IN IT!

Do you know that if we all put 3 inches less water in our bath, many thousands of tons of coal will be saved for war production in a year?

Never have more than 5 inches of water in your bath.

See what *you* can do about it. Start today.

Release
MORE COAL
FOR THE
WAR DRIVE

Shopping in Blackpool

If you were to ask what was one of my main wartime memories I would say queuing – standing in long queues, sometimes starting outside the door of the shop, for quite ordinary things. One of these was fish, but Blackpool was lucky for it was close to the port of Fleetwood and fish was only really short in the storms of winter.

Occasionally luxury items, such as oranges, would arrive and we would join a long queue hoping that supplies would not run out before our turn arrived. Housewives usually carried a string bag in their handbag just in case!

I don't remember seeing a banana until 1946, and rumour had it that when they were first available children thought that one ate the skin as well.

Clothes were a constant problem, particularly for a parent trying to clothe a fast-growing child. Here my main memory is twofold. The first is of clothes which were bought large and 'turned up' and then gradually let down. These were much preferable to my second memory of 'hand-me-downs' – clothes from adult relatives which were then adjusted for a growing boy.

At this time there were no supermarkets. How long each day do you think it would have taken to search for the basic foods that you eat as a matter of course? How many different shops would you have had to go to?

Even hot water had to be used sparingly.

Ration books became part of everyone's lives.

THINGS TO DO

1 *Dig for Victory* was a popular slogan. Find out what it means. Devise a poster to support this slogan, or another urging people to eat more vegetables.

2 Look at the points allocated for clothes and at the advertisements. Try and work out how you would have managed, by giving a points score to all your clothing.

3 Why do you think that rationing led to people eating more healthi-ly during the war? List what you ate yesterday and then circle foods which were not essential – e.g. chocolate.

4 Why did the Ministry of Food believe that the points system was a much more flexible scheme? N.B. The points needed for each item could vary, and changes were given in the newspapers by the Ministry of Food.

CAN YOU WORK OUT ?

the meaning of 'spivs', black market and 'under the counter' in the last paragraph of page 36?

Why do they not exist today?

HOW VICTORY WAS ACHIEVED

The Government had planned for a three year war in 1939 but it was to last twice that time before Germany, and finally Japan, were defeated. A child starting school in September 1939 would have been in secondary school in the year the war ended. Looking back it seemed only a matter of time before the Germans were defeated, but this was not the case.

After the fall of France in 1940 Britain stood alone. Western Europe was in German hands and few gave much for Britain's chances. In May 1940 Neville Chamberlain was replaced by Winston Churchill as Prime Minister, the month that the evacuation of Dunkirk took place. This did much for morale, but within weeks the Germans had entered Paris in triumph.

At home the Blitz had begun, and Britain now knew that it was at war. Rationing was introduced, signposts, street signs and station names were all removed and a second evacuation began.

On the positive side, the bravery of British pilots during the Battle of Britain, and the way in which the civilian population refused to be beaten during the bombing of the major cities, did much for morale, as well as uniting the people as never before.

By 1941 Britain was on a full war footing and there were necessary wartime restrictions which affected everyone – from blackouts to identity cards and ration books. At sea the German submarines were attacking ships bringing valuable supplies from North America, while on land Rommel was becoming a legendary German Commander, as he swept through North Africa.

It is against this background that we should read Churchill's speeches and admire the way that he went out into the bombed areas, and visited the troops at the Front.

Hitler's failure to win the Battle of Britain and then the suspension of his invasion plans led him to launch his invasion of the Soviet Union in June 1941. Again he nearly succeeded and might have done if he had begun a month earlier. However, Britain now had the most unexpected of allies – Communist Russia under Joseph Stalin. The British public were now persuaded that kindly 'Uncle Joe' was leading a heroic people against the German invaders. This was true, although Stalin was in his own way as ruthless a leader as Hitler.

The other turning point of the war was the surprise air attack by Japanese fighter planes on the American base at Pearl Harbor in Hawaii on 7 December 1941. Not only did it bring the USA into the war against Japan but also into the European war against Hitler. Nevertheless, 1942 was a hard year for the British public and shortages of fuel, food and transport continued. Abroad there were defeats in North Africa until Montgomery turned the tide at El Alamein.

From then on there were victories and Churchill's position as Prime Minister was secure. American soldiers (known as GIs – 'Government Issue') arrived in Britain in 1942, and in the following year the Allies landed in Sicily. After much hard fighting, Italy surrendered.

War meant that traditional roles were abandoned. Here, women make shells in an armaments factory.

Your **BRITAIN** · *fight for it now*

Stalin had been calling for a second front to relieve the pressure on Russia, and this was finally to come in June 1944, with the Allied Invasion of Normandy. German resistance was stubborn and the British public were subjected to the new German secret weapons – the V1s and V2s which caused many deaths and further evacuations.

Victory against Germany (VE Day) came in May 1945 but it took several more months, and the use of two atomic bombs, before Japan surrendered in August 1945 (VJ Day).

The war had cost many lives but had seen the British united as never before. Churchill, a Conservative, had been prime minister of a government drawn from all the major parties. In the last few years of the war government reports had been produced which laid the foundation for the Education Act of 1944 and the future Welfare State. No one wanted to go back to the poverty and high unemployment of the inter-war years.

Propaganda posters such as this one encouraged the population to continue the fight.

Their Finest Hour

The Battle of France is over. I expect that the Battle of Britain is about to begin. The whole fury and might of the enemy must very soon be turned on us. Hitler knows that he will have to break us in this island or lose the war. If we can stand up to him, all Europe may be free and the life of the world may move forward . . . But if we fail, then the whole world including the United States . . . will sink into the abyss of a new Dark Age . . . Let us therefore brace ourselves to our duties, and so bear ourselves that, if the British Empire and Commonwealth last for a thousand years, men will still say – 'This was their finest hour'.

(Winston Churchill, 18 June 1940)

A dogfight over Kent

'There's one coming down in flames – there somebody's hit a German – and he's coming down – there's a long stream – he's coming down completely out of petrol – a long streak of smoke – ah, the man's baled out by parachute – the pilot's baled out by parachute – he's a Junker 87 and he's going straight into the sea and there he goes – sma-a-sh – Oh, boy, I've never seen anything so good as this – the RAF fighters have really got these boys taped.'

(Charles Gardner, BBC reporter 10, July, 1940, quoted by A. Calder, *The People's War*, 1972)

Do you think that reports and speeches such as these boosted morale?

Victory celebrations in Leicester Square, London.

The war over, millions of conscripts went back to 'civvy street'.

TIME CHART

		At home		Abroad
1939	May	Conscription for 20–21 year-olds if war breaks out, then 18–21.	23 Aug.	Nazi-Soviet Non-Aggression Pact.
			25 Aug.	Britain and Poland sign treaty of mutual assistance.
	1 Sept.	First evacuation 1.5 million. Anderson shelters are distributed.	1 Sept.	Germany invades Poland.
		Civil Defence called to their posts. Ration books issued.	3 Sept	Britain, France, Australia, New Zealand declare war on Germany.
			28 Sept.	Poland surrenders.
1940	Jan.–Feb.	Coldest winter for 45 years – Thames frozen for eight miles.	9 April	Germany invades Denmark and Norway.
	8 Jan.	Butter and sugar rationed.	10 May	Germany invades Holland, Belgium and Luxembourg.
	10 May	Winston Churchill replaces Neville Chamberlain as Prime Minister.	15 May	Holland surrenders.
	14 May	Local Defence Force formed.	26 May–4 June	Evacuation from Dunkirk.
	May–June	Bombing begins – 2nd evacuation.	28 May	Belgium surrenders.
	July	Tea, margarine, cooking fats rationed.	16 July	Hitler orders preparations for invasion of Britain.
	10 July	Battle of Britain begins.		
	7 Sept.	Blitz begins.	17 Sept.	Operation Sea Lion (invasion) plans cancelled.
	29 Dec.	London fire-bombed ('Second Fire of London').		
1941	May	Blitz ends.	22 June	Germany invades Russia.
			7 Dec.	Japan bombs Pearl Harbor.
				Russia and USA join the Allies.
1942		Year of further shortages – no petrol for pleasure.		
	Jan.	First GIs arrive.		
	Feb.	Soap ration: 16 oz for 4 weeks.	7–15 March	Singapore captured by the Japanese.
	April	Exeter, Bath, Norwich, York bombed.		
	6 April	No more white bread.		
	May–June	Canterbury bombed.		
	July	Chocolates and sweets rationed at 8oz for 4 weeks.	4 July	First US bombing raids on Germany.
	Sept.	Clothes coupons reduced to 48 a year (handkerchief 3 coupons).	4 Nov.	Victory at El Alamein by Montgomery.

	At home		Abroad	
1943		Six million fireguards working 48 hours a month.	Jan.	Surrender of Germans at Stalingrad.
	Summer	Twice as many women in work as in 1918.	10 July	Allied forces landed in Sicily.
		750,000 in Home Guard.	Dec.	RAF bomb Berlin.
1944	Jan.	The Little Blitz on London.		
	13 June	First V Bomb launched against Britain (Flying Bombs).	6 June	Allied landing in Normandy.
	8 Sept.	V2s launched by Germany (45 feet long, 14 tons weight).		
			13 Sept.	Allies enter Germany.
			16 Dec–16 Jan. 1945	Battle of the Bulge – last German offensive.
1945	28 March	Last of 1050 V Bombs falls.	26 April	US and Soviet troops meet at the Elbe.
			30 April	Suicide of Hitler.
	8 May	VE Day.	7 May	German unconditional surrender.
	July	Labour landslide victory – Attlee becomes Prime Minister.	6 Aug.	Atomic bomb dropped on Hiroshima, Japan.
			9 Aug.	Atomic bomb dropped on Nagasaki, Japan.
	2 Sept.	VJ Day.	14 Aug.	Japan surrenders.
			20 Nov.	War trials of German leaders at Nuremburg.

GLOSSARY

Anderson Shelter	Family shelter constructed in the garden
Armourer	Maker or repairer of weapons
Artefact	Object made by man
Auxiliary services	Services which helped the full-time ones
Barrage balloon	Large static balloons raised above towns to impede enemy aircraft
Black Market	Selling goods illegally at a higher price, (e.g. without coupons)
Blackout	After sunset all lights had to be covered so as not to aid enemy aircraft
Camaraderie	Friendly sociability
Civilian(s)	People at home, as opposed to being in the Armed Forces
Civvies	Ordinary clothes worn by servicemen on leave
Civvy Street	Civilian life to which servicemen returned after the war
Control Post	The command centre for Civil Defence
Cower	To crouch down in fear
Dogfight	Air battle between opposing aircraft
Mickey Mouse gas mask	A child's gas mask
Pint	A liquid measure
Reconnaissance	An initial survey before attack
Retaliate	To strike back
Spivs	Those who made their money illegally
Splendour	Magnificence

Abbreviations

AFS	Auxiliary Fire Service
APC	Auxiliary Police Constable
ARP	Air Raid Precautions
BBC	British Broadcasting Corporation
BEF	British Expeditionary Force
CD	Civil Defence
GI	General Issue
HG	Home Guard
HMSO	His Majesty's Stationary Office
MOF	Ministry of Food
NCO	Non-Commissioned Officer
RAF	Royal Air Force
RAOC	Royal Army Ordnance Corps
VE	Victory Europe
VJ	Victory Japan
WVS	Women's Voluntary Service

What Can You Remember?

Why was the Bore War so named?

How was the evacuation from Dunkirk undertaken?

What part was played by Radar and the RAOC in the Battle of Britain?

When did the Blitz begin and how long did it last?

Where was the BBC first evacuated?

Why were ARP wardens both useful and disliked?

What did the Civil Defence forces do?

Why were you warned not to go sightseeing after an Air Raid?

What did the LDV later become?

What was an Anderson Shelter?

What did Chislehurst caves and the London Underground have in common?

What was Points Rationing?

Why was the wartime diet healthy?

How did Britain celebrate her victories over Germany and Japan?

PLACES TO VISIT

Age Concern Reminiscence Centre, Blackheath, London. Displays and documents. People come here to share their memories. (Books sold include: *Fifty Years Ago* and *What did you do in the War, Mum?*)

Cabinet War Room, Horse Guards Road, London. The underground rooms which were the nerve centre of Britain's defence and where Churchill had safe accommodation.

Duxford Air Museum, Duxford, Cambridgeshire. Former RAF wartime airfield covers 70 years of aviation history.

Eden Camp, Malton, North Yorkshire. The story of civilian life during the Second World War.

Imperial War Museum, Lambeth Road, London. A museum of the twentieth century. Contains important sections on the domestic front. Contains a fine poster and photographic section.

Museum of London, London Wall, London. Contains sections on the Second World War.

Watford Museum, High Street, Watford, Herts. One of many local museums which have good displays on life in the Second World War.

FURTHER READING

Jones, M. V., *Life in Britain in World War II*, Batsford, 1983

Longmate, N., *How We Lived Then: A History of Everyday Life During the Second World War*, Hutchinson, 1971

Merson, E., *Children in the Second World War*, Longman, 1988

Minns, R., *Bombers and Mash*, Virago, 1980

Tooth, C., *Evacuation*, Tressell, 1989

Tyson, N. L., *Growing Up in the Second World War*, Batsford, 1981

Acknowledgments

The Author and Publishers would like to thank the following for permission to reproduce illustrations: The Hulton Picture Co. for pages 12, 13, 16–17, 32, 39, 40, 42; The Imperial War Museum for pages 5, 7, 9, 15, 19, 22, 23, 26, 28, 30, 34, 35; The Kent Messenger Group for page 11; London Transport for page 18; Mr Bill Morton for page 31. The pictures were researched by David Pratt.

INDEX

Numbers in **bold type** refer to illustrations